## Bible Study

7 SESSIONS FOR SMALL GROUP AND PERSONAL USE

# Revive Your Church

Seeking and Encountering Abundant Life

Copyright © Waverley Abbey Trust, 2023.

Published 2023 by Waverley Abbey Trust, Waverley Abbey House, Waverley Lane, Farnham, Surrey GU9 8EP, UK. Registered Charity No. 294387. Registered limited company No. 1990308.

The right of Terry Hart to be identified as the author of this work has been asserted by him in accordance with the Copyright, Designs and Patents Act 1988, sections 77 and 78.

All rights reserved. No part of this publication may be reproduced, stored in a retrieval system, or transmitted, in any form or by any means, electronic, mechanical, photocopying, recording or otherwise, without the prior permission in writing of Waverley Abbey Resources.

For a list of National Distributors, visit waverleyabbeytrust.org/distributors

Unless otherwise indicated, all Scripture references are from the NIV, New International Version® Anglicised, NIV® Copyright © 1979, 1984, 2011 by Biblica, Inc.® Used by permission. All rights reserved worldwide.

Other Bible translations: NKJV, Scripture taken from the New King James Version®. Copyright © 1982 by Thomas Nelson. Used by permission. All rights reserved.

Every effort has been made to ensure that this book contains the correct permissions and references, but if anything has been inadvertently overlooked, the Publisher will be pleased to make the necessary arrangements at the first opportunity. Please contact the Publisher directly.

Concept development and editing by Waverley Abbey Trust.

Design and typesetting by Richard Lyall.

Printed and bound in the UK.

Paperback ISBN: 978-1-78951-441-4

Ebook ISBN: 978-1-78951-505-3

# Contents

| | |
|---|---|
| 4 | INTRODUCTION TO THE COVER TO COVER SERIES |
| 6 | ABOUT THE AUTHOR |
| 7 | INTRODUCTION |
| 11 | WEEK ONE<br>**Humble Themselves** |
| 17 | WEEK TWO<br>**Pray and Seek** |
| 23 | WEEK THREE<br>**And Turn Away** |
| 29 | WEEK FOUR<br>**Be Reclaimed** |
| 35 | WEEK FIVE<br>**Be Repaired** |
| 41 | WEEK SIX<br>**Be Alive** |
| 47 | WEEK SEVEN<br>**Awaken Others** |
| 53 | LEADER'S NOTES |
| 73 | DAILY GUIDE |

# About Cover to Cover

The *Cover to Cover* Bible Study Guides are a popular series helping individuals and groups to engage with the Bible and to dig deeper.

The first studies were produced in 2002 by Selwyn Hughes and now cover more than 80 different themes, characters and books of the Bible, and are compiled by various writers and Bible teachers.

# How to Get the Best from the Studies

The *Cover to Cover* studies are designed to be either worked through individually or in a group. Whichever way you are using the study we encourage you to begin with prayer, asking God through His Holy Spirit to work in your life through these studies. Then trust that He will!

Do allow enough time for the questions and exercises, not rushing through but allocating time to focus on questions that raise specific challenges.

If you are studying as a group you may find our online resources useful. Here you will find some extra video content and copies of the daily guide to distribute to the members. Visit **wvly.org/c2ccv** to discover what is available.

In group discussions do make use of the leader's notes at the end of the study. Ensure that you give everyone in the group time to share and avoid allowing one person to dominate conversation.

Please feel free to adapt the material according to your group's needs. Trust that God is with you, leading you and helping each one of you draw closer to Him.

# About the Author

## Written by Terry Hart

**Terry Hart** has a background in secondary education; teaching and leading Religious Education. He is an Adviser on Religious Education and Christian Distinctiveness in Church Schools. Terry is also a Pastor in the Free Methodist Church and church planter of 'Revive FMC' in Oldham, England.

# Introduction

Christian revival is the exhibition of God's power, witnessed and embraced. It is a period of awe and wonder, where people recognise the majesty of God. It is not initiated or engineered by humankind, nor the product of good works, but the releasing of His power in His time.

When picturing a revival, imagination may create an image of churches that are full, score upon score of new believers coming before God for the first time and people genuinely giving their lives in totality to Jesus Christ, their saviour. There, the Holy Spirit would be gifting people afresh and the whole of the body of Christ would be bearing the fruit of the Spirit. It would be a time of transformation with the potential to heal communities, countries and the whole of creation.

However, though revival is a wonder, imagination may not produce a true picture of exactly what revival is. The above outlines something that would be better described as a great awakening. This is the period of time that often follows a period of revival, brought about by the events of the revival itself.

In 2 Chronicles 7:14 it states 'if my people, who are called by my name, will humble themselves and pray and seek my face and turn from their wicked ways, then I will hear from heaven, and I will forgive their sin and will heal their land.' It is this relationship between the seeking and the saving, the preparing and the pouring that is often provides a true reflection of revival.

Revival is when people seek and experience the abundant life that Jesus offers. Not simply life eternal, but a fullness of life in the now; through the experiencing of God, through the power of the Holy Spirit, the making known of this in the receiving of gifts and the bearing of fruit. Awakening is the knowledge of Jesus as Lord, but being revived is the living of life in God, through Jesus, empowered by the Spirit.

The Bible provides the basis for an understanding of revival in moments such as the return of the exiles and the rebuilding of the Temple in Ezra 3, the breathing of life into the valley of dry bones in Ezekiel 37 and the transformational experience of the Spirit at Pentecost in Acts 2, which saw the filling and empowering of individuals, the evidence of gifting afresh, the renewal of the believer, the proclaiming of the gospel, and the birth of the Church. These biblical examples of revival are both personal and corporate. Revival doesn't need a huge crowd; it could simply begin with a remnant of His people, though once it begins an overpouring will follow.

The history books record many revivals in the United Kingdom and America through the seventeenth and eighteenth centuries. These are often described as 'Awakenings', where the increased desire to experience a closeness to God was reflected in religious fervency and presented itself in behavioural change. These usually came in response to an observation made by many that they were in a time of stepping away from God and the scripturally moral foundations which Christianity had provided for society.

In eighteenth-century Britain, John and Charles Wesley had been led to a deeper and more authentic relationship with God, which had brought about a desire for holiness, but this was enhanced when John experienced a personal revival moment. John's heart was moved by the Spirit during a reading of Luther's preface to the book of Romans; he received assurance of his faith and conviction in his desire to do God's work.

INTRODUCTION

Combined with the way God had moved George Whitfield, these personal revivals joined with many others and created a revival movement: preaching outdoors, churches planted, preachers called, thousands having their faith restored and thousands more coming to faith for the first time. Social change followed, with many recognising the Wesleyan Revival as one of the contributing factors of the abolition of slavery in the United Kingdom.

A more recent revival is the 1904–1905 Welsh Revival. God used Evan Roberts, a man who had longed for revival for thirteen years. Roberts was a preacher who, though many would say was not a gifted speaker, enthralled congregations with his faith, love and passion for the power of the Holy Spirit. God responded to a people who were passionate in prayer, authentic in worship, enthusiastic in study and confident in the sharing of their testimony with an outpouring of the Holy Spirit. Christians were revived in their faith and 70,000 new people came to know Jesus in the first three months. There was an overwhelming sense of the presence of God at this time. Debts were paid, policemen were not needed, relationships were healed, hymns were sung at football matches, theatres and bars were empty and the churches were full.

These revivals followed the pattern of the scriptural account of revival and started with an individual desiring to be filled, and willing to be emptied. As church attendance drops, as society battles need against want, as fashions fuel greed and envy, as the world is threatened by poverty, conflict and climate change, revival is needed more than ever.

As we have read, revival is often a corporate state, a movement across a people, but it starts with the individual believer. This study aims to provide a better understanding of revival in the Bible and in history through highlighting not events, but the process of transformation – the change found in those who are moved by revival and those who are then changed as witnesses. Completing this Bible study will not simply flick the switch that brings about revival, but it is hoped it will provide some preparation by being able to identify revival, by preparing hearts and minds for revival, by restoring the Church's desire for spiritual revival and by creating in individuals a longing to be revived and return to the closeness of God they have experienced and desire that for others also.

WEEK ONE
# Humble Themselves

## Opening Exercise

Being humbled has been identified as a key step towards revival.

When have you felt humbled? Why was this?

## Bible Readings

- 2 Chronicles 7:11–22
- John 3:30
- Romans 3:23
- Philippians 2:3–11
- 1 Peter 5:6

## Key Verse

'If my people, who are called by my name, will humble themselves and pray and seek my face and turn from their wicked ways, then I will hear from heaven, and I will forgive their sin and will heal their land' (2 Chr. 7:14).

## Focus

The need to humble ourselves before God heals the land.

## Opening Our Eyes

The preacher was in his mid-eighties and walked with a stick for support. The front of the church had been adapted somewhat with additional rails and more manageable steps. All of this was done to allow the older members to take a seat at the platform to lead worship and prayer. When at the point of the sermon, the preacher rose to his feet, stepped down from the platform using the rails to support him and reached back for his stick. He started to shuffle away from the platform towards the pulpit, then, one step at a time, he pulled himself up the steps, again using rails and his stick to support him until he reached the top. Though out of breath and unsteady, he began to preach. A humbling moment for any preacher present, that one of their number would be so obedient, and reverential of the Word that the necessity for its sharing and status would outweigh their own physical difficulties.

We may reflect on moments of feeling humbled as positive encounters. We consider that feeling or rush of emotion when we are humbled as a pleasing instance; perhaps it is provoked by the charity of another, their selflessness or generosity. Often in these cases we see the positive impact of another's behaviour either for ourselves or for someone we love. This, again, can cause some to believe that being humbled is a pleasant experience resulting in immediate gain. However, we see in Scripture that God desires His people to be humble and that, in the most part, they are not.

In 2 Chronicles 7, King Solomon humbled himself by taking all of the focus directed to him as king and placing it before God. Solomon used the vast resources made available to him. There

## HUMBLE THEMSELVES

were thousands of talents of gold, millions of talents of silver and unmeasurable amounts of copper and iron. Wood piles and quarried stone too great to count, as well as unnumbered craftsmen. Solomon committed the resources to the will of God, rather than his own glory. He built a temple for God and, in doing so, his people were humbled before God as they knelt on the ground and turned their faces to the floor.

Humbling oneself is not simply an Old Testament practice. Jesus too humbled those who observed Him living out God's plan on earth. The crowd who held stones and called for punishment were humbled of their status as He suggested those free from sin should throw the first stone at the adulterous woman. They were humbled to the point that they walked away. Paul also continued this approach as he stated in his letter to the Romans that all have sinned and fallen short of the glory of God. This form of being humbled is very different from the fuzzy sense of emotion we often experience. It is the holding up of a mirror, a recognition of sin and our human nature that very quickly resets our view of ourselves and our position, placing God in his rightful place.

The moment of humbling caused by the elderly preacher was so, not because it reflected his goodness, but because it highlighted a potential lacking in the observer. Those who were present found themselves asking, 'Would I, could I, do that?' It is the highlighting of this potential lacking that brings about the steps towards humility.

## Discussion Starters

1. How has God called you? What changes have you seen in your life?

2. What did Solomon do to humble himself?

3. How can we humble ourselves? How will this humility impact upon our behaviour?

4. Considering our sin can be a challenging and difficult process. Why is it necessary to accept Paul's statement that 'all have sinned' (Rom. 3:23)?

HUMBLE THEMSELVES

5. Where can we seek the face of God? Where has he revealed Himself to us?

6. How is humbling ourselves related to us receiving God's forgiveness?

7. How might being humble enable us to be more forgiving?

8. Where do we need God's healing in our land? How could God use us to bring about this healing? How will being humble help us to complete God's work?

## Personal Application

How then can we seek to be a humble people? Not through the actions of others, but our own. It cannot be done simply to seek a movement of God, as its sincerity is questionable. Nor can it be done in one swift moment; developing humility is a process. Thankfully Scripture provides us with examples and guidance to do this. With those already provided in mind, and perhaps others you have found, consider the following:

- Your gifts have come from God. We have nothing to be proud of, and everything to be thankful for.
- You are a sinner. Consider your sins, in every part of your life, and ask for forgiveness (as often as needed.)
- Serve others without seeking anything in return.
- Direct all glory to God.
- Do not seek to please people, only God.
- Pray, as you are dependent on Him.

Is there a particular point that you could focus on as you seek to be humbled before God? Does any of this challenge you now and need your focus in prayer, study and reflection?

## Seeing Jesus in the Scriptures

The necessity for humility is a constant thread throughout Scripture. Joseph, son of Jacob was made humble through his period of separation from belongings and status. David humbled himself through the writing of the psalms and recognition of God's glory. Solomon humbled himself through the sacrifice of resources and time while seeking to create a worthy house for God, so much greater than his own. Jesus humbled himself through service to others and spending time with those whom society saw as unclean or sinners. Jesus also provided us with the parable of the pharisee and the tax collector, recorded in Luke 18:9–14, to illustrate humility to us.

WEEK TWO

# Pray and Seek

## Opening Exercise

Has there been a time when you have felt a desperate need to pray? Why was this? How did praying change you, others and the situation you were praying for?

## Bible Readings

- 2 Chronicles 7:11–22
- Habakkuk
- Psalm 80
- Psalm 85:1–7

## Key Verse

'Lord, I have heard of your fame; I stand in awe of your deeds, Lord. Repeat them in our day, in our time make them known; in wrath remember mercy' (Hab. 3:1–2, NIV).

'O Lord, I have heard Your speech and was afraid; O Lord, revive Your work in the midst of the years! In the midst of the years make it known; in wrath remember mercy' (NKJV).

## Focus

The need to become a prayerful people before God heals the land.

## Opening Our Eyes

On 27 February 2022, the Church of England observed a day of prayer. This day of prayer was called by Justin Welby, the Archbishop of Canterbury in response to the conflict in Ukraine. Pope Francis responded to the conflict by declaring a day of prayer on Ash Wednesday 2022. Such calls to pray were not new events. On 26 May 1940, during the Second World War, King George VI called for a day of prayer as the British Expeditionary Forces became overwhelmed by German forces. Around a third of a million soldiers faced death or capture and retreated to northern France. Similar days of prayer were called by George V in the First World War and further days were called during the Second World War. Why was this?

There seems to be a pattern that, during times of national or international crisis, people turn to God in prayer. It is when the alternatives have been exhausted, when hope is faltering and when the potential for failure or defeat means a future of pain or suffering, that people turn to the greatest power. There is perhaps a question over why we wait for the crisis before we turn to prayer but, regardless of this, there is evidence in these actions of the knowledge of God's awesome power. As prayers have been answered, the glory has then been given to God.

In session one we explored how humility is a recognition of the ultimate power of God. This understanding of God's power and His plan allows us to place all glory at His feet rather than claiming success for ourselves, but this revelation also provokes a new reliance on God and His plan. This reliance is seen through a commitment to prayer.

## PRAY AND SEEK

A key element of revival through history and Scripture is the hearts of the people becoming passionate about prayer. Not just praying to communicate with God and further develop their relationship with Him, but to develop such a closeness that it is His will that is desired.

Habakkuk was lamenting during a time when God's law was being neglected, when there was conflict and injustice. Not only this, but Israel's southern kingdom faced attack from the Babylonians, whom Habakkuk regarded as being even worse enemies. Habakkuk lay his woes before God and longed for the days when the kingdom would recognise God's sovereignty. However, God revealed a plan that would not be a return to the past but a new future. God revealed that He would in fact use the Babylonians in a way almost akin to cleansing the kingdom. Habakkuk was not happy with the reply and complained, then God replied again confirming His intentions. At this point Habakkuk turned to prayer. He accepted God's will and prayed it into being, praying for mercy in God's action and, in this, humbling himself as unworthy. He then ended his prayer by rejoicing in the Lord.

Habakkuk's prayer reflects an urgency for a resolution and a plea to God to restore, but in his prayerful behaviour he becomes accepting of God's plan and also prays that God's will be done. No longer arguing for his nation's restoration alone, as he is humbled before God, he prays for God's mercy and declares God as his source of strength and his abilities. In Psalms 80 and 85 we read the words 'restore us O God' and 'revive us'. These pleas are not a desire to necessarily return to a certain time or situation, but to a state of being, that of being a Spirit-filled people, who recognise His authority and yearn for His will and His kingdom. Prayer then is a key element in being revived, while being prayerful is also evidence of being revived. In this way, prayer is not simply a process by which to achieve an end, but also an end in itself. Becoming entirely prayer-driven and reliant on Him is a blessing in itself.

 ## Discussion Starters

1. How might a person seek God's face? How could prayer be part of this process?

2. What might a prayerful person be like?

3. Why is Habakkuk's opening of 'O Lord...' significant?

4. What does Habakkuk 3:18 say about the change in his approach to God?

PRAY AND SEEK

5. How does Psalm 80 compare with Habakkuk's prayer?

6. Has there been a time when your prayers have changed from a desire for your will to a desire for His? How did this change you in your approach to prayer?

7. How might our longing for God's plan be seen in our behaviours?

8. What can we pray for ourselves and our church in preparation for revival?

## Personal Application

Seeking is an intentional behaviour; it is the dedication of time and resources and will probably also involve sacrifice. The motivation comes from a desire to find the thing you seek. Deuteronomy makes this point in 4:29, 'But if from there you seek the Lord your God, you will find him if you seek him with all your heart and with all your soul.' There are many Hebrew words in Scripture that relate to the word 'seek', but a general definition would be to 'search out by any method'. The next step then is to explore the methods available in searching out God and His will for you, your church and the wider community. Consider the following questions:

1. What change would be needed for you to become a prayerful person?
2. What could your church do to support people in seeking to become prayerful?
3. How might these changes impact on you and your local church community?

## Seeing Jesus in the Scriptures

Jesus was dedicated to prayer. Some have questioned why Jesus prayed; one of the reasons given is that Jesus was setting us an example of how to stay in close communion with God. Jesus often took himself away to prayer, removing distractions and providing himself with time and focus before His Father. The Gospels tell us of times when Jesus left early in the morning to pray alone (Mark 1:35), or when he would take a different path to the disciples in order to have prayer time (Mark 6:46). Jesus would also pray through the night (Luke 6:12). His prayer life led him to that point in the garden of Gethsemane where He would declare, 'yet not my will, but yours be done' (Luke 22:42). Acts 1:14 tells us that those in the early Church followed Christ's example and often prayed together as a community.

WEEK THREE
# And Turn Away

## Opening Exercise

Life has lots of movement – from moving house, to changing job to becoming a parent. These changes can have a positive and/or negative impact upon a person. What major changes have you had in your life? How have these had an impact on you and those around you?

## Bible Readings

- Genesis 3
- Exodus 20:1–17
- 2 Chronicles 7:11–22
- John 14:21
- Acts 3:19

## Key Verse

'Repent, then, and turn to God, so that your sins may be wiped out, that times of refreshing may come from the Lord' (Acts 3:19).

## Focus

The need to acknowledge sin, confess and repent.

## Opening Our Eyes

Acts 3:19 tells us that in preparation for a time of refreshing, a turn to God for the removal of sin is needed. Therefore, a step towards being revived is acknowledging that our need for revival is due to sin. If we were all walking faithfully along the path the Lord had laid, we would not need revival. The kingdom would be established on earth. The next step towards being revived, therefore, is to go through a continuous process of confession.

The verses from 2 Chronicles 7 state that God desires us to turn away from our wicked ways. This suggests a complete change in the direction of our lives. God cannot be found in the way of wickedness, hence the need to turn away from this to seek His face. If we are headed in the direction of wickedness, then we have turned our backs on God.

Sin has been creating a barrier between God and His creation since the Fall. The serpent came to Eve and asked, 'did God really say' (Gen. 3:1) and this question has been casting a shadow of a mixture of doubt and false confidence into the thought patterns of humankind ever since. Humans have either doubted the authority, or even existence, of God or have had too much confidence in their actions to convict them of their validity, convincing themselves that their behaviours are acceptable.

As we saw in Week One, Paul taught that 'all have sinned and fall short of the glory of God' (Rom. 3:23). This highlights the fragile state of humankind and the continuing impact of the Fall. It also reflects the absolute need for the crucifixion of Jesus, to save us from the sin in the world. It is hoped that Paul's point provokes a person to explore a time of humility, fuelled by a drive to pray and a desire to confess and repent. Confession itself, is a mark of humility. To confess means to admit, or to agree, that you are a sinner.

However, it is worth noting that, though we might happily accept that all are sinners, it is easy to fall into a condition where we do not recognise all our own acts as sin. We can start evaluating our own behaviour, defining what is sin and what isn't. Excuses such as, 'that small lie made someone feel better', 'everybody else was doing it', 'it was fun', 'it didn't harm anyone' and 'I'm only human' can make us feel better about our behaviours. These excuses downplay the impact of sin in our lives. They create a state of self-absolution and bypass Scripture and, most of all, bypass the cross. If there were no sin, there would have been no need for the crucifixion.

Another risk for Christians, highlighted in Romans 6, is to cheapen grace. This can be done by embracing salvation to the extent that any behaviour is acceptable because we have been washed in the blood of Jesus and therefore have been forgiven of all sin. This reduces our relationship with our saviour to a one-time act of kindness rather than an ongoing act of reconciliation and reparation of humankind's relationship with their Father.

Scripture provides us with lots of instruction as to what is sinful and therefore using Scripture is key to identifying sin, confessing of it and repenting. To do this, it is appropriate to read over the Ten Commandments in Exodus 20 to recall how God has called us to love Him and love each other. John 14:21 states that the following of God's commands, not simply knowing of them, is the way to show our love towards God. It is also worthwhile exploring Paul's letters and his highlighting of behaviours that should be avoided.

## Discussion Starters

1. What is sin? It might be useful to think of some examples and find where in the Bible we are told each one is sinful.

2. What were the consequences of Adam and Eve's behaviours? Are the consequences the same for us?

3. Why did God give His commandments? Do they still apply?

4. How is sin damaging to humankind?

AND TURN AWAY

5. What is required of us to successfully turn our back on sin?

6. Is it possible to avoid sin and still be reaching out into the world?

7. How do we teach others about sin without being judgemental?

8. How might we support others in avoiding sin?

## Personal Application

What can you do to help yourself avoid sin?

- Read your Bible.
- Learn to love what God loves, and discover the fun in following His passions. Explore things you can enjoy while following God. Find a niche area of outreach. within your church that matches your passions or pray for a new passion to match the need.
- Sin can be enticing so construct limits in your life. Be aware of the triggers to sin and avoid them. Draw lines in the sand for the situations or bad influences you will avoid or walk away from.
- Pray through temptation. Ask yourself: is this behaviour honouring to God? Use the Lord's Prayer to steady yourself and regain focus on God's will.
- Build accountability into your life with the help of a small group, prayer partner or trusted Christian friend.

There will be other ways to approach the issue of sin, temptation, confession and repentance. However the process is undertaken, it is a key process in order to be open to a revival in your life and community.

## Seeing Jesus in the Scriptures

Jesus experienced the trial of temptation but did not sin (Matt. 4:1–11). How did He do this? Jesus used Scripture to protect Himself. He kept His focus on God and God's will. Jesus knew when He had to say no and tell Satan to leave Him alone. Jesus then allowed the angels to tend to Him. So what can we learn from Jesus on the topic of sin? 'But if we were more discerning with regard to ourselves, we would not come under such judgment' (1 Corinthians 11:31). We need to be clear what sin is and avoid excuses for the sins we struggle with, then confess our sins and turn our face away from them.

WEEK FOUR
# Be Reclaimed

## Opening Exercise

Have you ever bought anything second-hand? What was it that attracted you to it? Why did you decide not to buy new?

## Bible Readings

- Psalm 139:13–18
- Luke 15:11–32
- Acts 16:31
- Ephesians 1:4–5
- 1 Peter 2:9

## Key Verse

'Believe in the Lord Jesus, and you will be saved' (Acts 16:31).

 ## Focus

God wants to reclaim His creation through the cross of Jesus.

 ## Opening Our Eyes

In a world that is steadily becoming more eco-conscious, reclamation is quite a popular, perhaps even fashionable, pursuit. In 2021, the most popular second-hand online shop had over 184 million users worldwide. People are willing to hand over their unwanted belongings. Maybe they are not in good condition anymore, or they do not meet a desired purpose, or perhaps people just want to replace them with something new. Meanwhile, there are others who are seeking out the original, the retro, the different. There is someone who will desire each discarded object; someone wanting to prepare a place for it. In some cases, it may be that the unwanted object is going to become the 'talking piece' or the feature item in a particular space. If a person wants it, they simply have to purchase it, or outbid any other interest.

In the beginning we were God's. Psalm 139 speaks of God creating us in the womb, of how He looked over us as He formed us and His plan for us was already being crafted. In Ephesians 1:4–5 we are told that God chose us and determined a path for each of us in line with His will. His will is to prosper His people. Jeremiah 29:11 says: '"For I know the plans I have for you," declares the Lord, "plans to prosper you and not to harm you, plans to give you hope and a future."' God's desire has always been for us to live life to its fullest, a life with a hope and a future.

But then we fell away from God, and we lost all hope and any chance of a future. Since the Fall of Adam and Eve, humankind has become enslaved by sin and therefore, as Paul explains, all of us, each and every one of us, have become sinners. Evil made a claim on our lives, which we accepted and therefore we were no longer God's. In the greatest act of love, God sent His Son, Jesus, to die for us and to reclaim us in His name. 1 Peter 2:9 refers to us as a chosen priesthood who were called out of the darkness. Through Jesus all can be reclaimed simply through believing in Him. Acts 16:31 tells us of the event where Paul and Silas were broken free from prison and said simply to their jailer, 'Believe in the Lord Jesus, and you will be saved'.

It is the offer of salvation that allows us to be reclaimed by God. John 3:16 is often seen as the gospel message in a single verse: 'For God so loved the world that he gave his one and only Son, that whoever believes in him shall not perish but have eternal life'. God has given His Son for our forgiveness; Jesus gave His life so that we might live. All we need to do is believe.

We may have been discarded by people or even society. We may not 'fit in' with the new fashion or be up to date or 'on trend'. We may not have the financial worth or desired beauty that our culture demands. We may not be able to keep up with technology or we may no longer meet the measure of what society values. Regardless of whether society wants us or not, God does. He wants to reclaim us as His for He sees our original purpose. He sees His plan for us and is ready to lead us back onto the path if we want it. He has paid the price for us. Through the death of His son Jesus Christ, we have been purchased for God and Satan has been outbid.

## Discussion Starters

1. What is meant by reclamation?

2. How can we come to be owned by another?

3. Who is to blame for our sin?

4. How do our lives reflect who we belong to?

BE RECLAIMED

5. Do you know the plan God has for your life? If not, how can you find out?

6. How can we be reclaimed? Do we have a choice?

7. How is being reclaimed a step towards being revived?

8. How will our lives be different if we are reclaimed by God?

## Personal Application

Take some time to reflect on this question: do you need to be reclaimed by God? We are not perfect, so we will sin, as we will only achieve full sanctification when we go to heaven. However, the nature and extent of our sinful behaviours are a measure of our spiritual need. By reflecting on our behaviours, we recognise where we have gone astray and where we need to change.

Have you developed a rhythm in your life that ensures Bible study, prayer, fellowship, and mercy – sharing your time and resources with those in need? Being reclaimed is not simply about turning away from sin, it is about turning toward God. What can you do to reflect this in your life?

## Seeing Jesus in the Scriptures

One of Jesus' most well-known parables is the parable of the prodigal son. Prodigal in this sense refers to the wasteful extravagance of the son's behaviour. This parable is also known as the 'parable of the lost son'. The son is lost to his sinful desires and adherence to a society that has different values – it only values him while he has material worth.

When the son returns to the father, he is reclaimed. The father runs to him with open arms and has sandals placed on his feet and a ring put on his finger. As soon as the son desired the life his father could provide, he regained status, value and dignity.

It was the son's choice both to leave and to return. If he had known of his father's response maybe he would have returned sooner. This teaching assures us of our Father's response. Humbling ourselves and responding once again to all God has done for us through Jesus will lead to us being enveloped in the arms of God and welcomed home again.

WEEK FIVE
# Be Repaired

## Opening Exercise

Things don't last forever. Some consumables are even produced with a built-in, limited life span to ensure people will have to replace them in time. There was a time when people were encouraged to 'make do and mend'. Have you had anything that you have got repaired? Why didn't you just replace it?

## Bible Readings

- Isaiah 44:1-5
- Ezekiel 37:1–14
- Luke 5:17–26
- Luke 8:40–56

## Key Verse

'So I prophesied as I was commanded. And as I was prophesying, there was a noise, a rattling sound, and the bones came together, bone to bone' (Ezek. 37:7).

REVIVE YOUR CHURCH

## Focus

We return to God broken, but He can repair the broken.

## Opening Our Eyes

Kintsugi is the Japanese practice of repairing broken objects, mainly pottery. 'Kin' translates as golden and 'tsugi' means re-joining. The process involves collecting all of the broken pieces and carefully exploring which part they are, how they fit together and then bringing them back together. Glue is used to join the pieces and string or tape can be used to hold the pieces in place while the repair sets. Then, gold dust or infused paint is added to cover the cracks and to highlight the individual fixes along the journey to being repaired.

Kintsugi began as a need to repair a tea bowl in a way that would be attractive. However the process has become a useful tool for representing how our imperfections and difficulties can be repaired by God and even reflect His beauty.

There are many biblical examples of God's desire to repair His people. Adam and Eve, ashamed of their nakedness, were clothed by God to ease their brokenness (Gen. 3:21). Elijah humbled himself and turned to God in prayer even in his anguish, and was attended to by angels who gave him food, drink and enabled his rest (1 Kgs 19:1–9). In the parable of the prodigal son, the son was so hungry he had turned to eating pig feed, but his father fed him with a fattened calf (Luke 15:11–32).

Ezekiel 37:1–14 describes a vision of a valley of dry bones, which represents how God would reclaim and repair Israel. Once an army, the piles of dry bones were about to be repaired by God. God began by asking Ezekiel whether it was possible, and Ezekiel accepted that only God could know this. We imagine that this army was a defeated army and yet even after all of the

## BE REPAIRED

time passed, God could still turn things around, as nothing is impossible for Him.

God used Ezekiel to bring about a restoring of the army. Rattling sounds were heard as bones began to reattach to bones. Skeletons formed and stood up. The skeletons gained tendons, flesh and were then covered in skin. The effects of death were removed, the decay reversed and the skin regrown. It was not only a physical reparation, though, but a return of the individual and collective purposes of the people. Raised as individual soldiers, to be a part of an army again. They were raised and repaired to stand individually but also to still be referred to in the collective as part of something greater – in this case, an army.

In verse 9 of Ezekiel 37, it states that this reparation was made, 'that they may live'. This was not a reparation to return to the lives that they had, but to simply live again. In this instance, though, as an army their death represented defeat, so their raising to life represented a victory.

Once the bones were standing God spoke again, not now 'dry bones' but called them, In verse 12, 'my people'. God had not only repaired and re-established them, but he had also reclaimed them as His own. Though a person may not return to the life they had, God can raise and repair people into a new life as His own.

We have been reclaimed as broken people. God desires to repair us; not simply to return us to the state we were in but to redefine our wholeness and provide us with a newness that reflects our value in Him but also our journey to repair. The memory of our previous brokenness can be used to support others as they face challenges in their own lives. Our past is not hidden; our repair is celebrated as evidence of His love for us.

# Discussion Starters

1. What can brokenness look like in a person's life?

2. Can anything ever be broken beyond repair?

3. Why does it sometimes feel like things have to become impossible for God to act?

4. How can the imagery of kintsugi be used to explain how God repairs His people?

5. How can repairs be celebrated?

## BE REPAIRED

6. Why did God raise the dry bones?

7. How did God use Ezekiel?

8. What was the order of the repair of the dry bones and how might that order be significant?

9. How might the order be significant?

10. What would saying, 'I belong to the Lord' mean to you?

## Personal Application

God used Ezekiel to speak to the dry bones. God's power was in the work, but also worked through Ezekiel. How might we be used by God today to bring about repair work in the lives of others? One possible way would be to follow the command given to Ezekiel and speak out to the broken. A powerful form of sharing has been found in testimony. Paul made good use of his testimony, sharing his road to Damascus event and the subsequent healing of his blindness in Acts 22.

There is no coincidence that much of the theme of testimony is that of a story of repair. An overview of a person's 'Christ story'; the 'before Jesus', how you came to know Jesus and the 'what has happened since', can illustrate the repairs God has made. This sharing can be the gold on the crack, the beauty found in the brokenness.

How have you been repaired by God and how can you share this with others? We will be exploring testimonies in the final week of this study. Try starting to write a brief testimony in answer to this question. (This is not your life journey with Jesus, just the highlights of your conversion.) You may wish to share this at the start of session seven.

## Seeing Jesus in the Scriptures

One of the main aspects of Jesus' ministry was the healing of the sick, which we can see in many examples of healing (for example, Luke 8:40–56). In Luke 5 we read of how Jesus healed a paralysed man. In this story of healing, Jesus asks a question similar to God's question in Ezekiel 37: 'Which is easier...' Jesus asks, before He does the impossible. Jesus 'repairs' the man physically, but he also reclaims him spiritually as He forgives his sins. We see a reclaiming also when Jesus calls the man, 'friend'.

WEEK SIX
# Be Alive

## Opening Exercise

It is quite fashionable in society to have a great desire to embrace life fully. Sayings such as, 'you only live once', 'live your best life' and 'live life to the full' are often used to encourage a different perspective on life – perhaps one that seeks adventure or steps out from the crowd. Has there ever been a time when you have felt truly alive? What was so special about that moment? Was it a time of adventure or stepping out?

## Bible Readings

- Luke 24:6
- John 1:1–4
- John 10:10
- Romans 6:3–11

## Key Verse

'He is not here; he has risen!' (Luke 24:6).

## Focus

Being able to stand, to move and to walk is not the same as being alive.

## Opening Our Eyes

What does it mean to be alive? There are various definitions of being alive. The most basic definition would be simply to say that something is 'not dead'; there is some movement, some ongoing connection, seen or unseen. Around 20% of people suffer from thanatophobia, which is the general fear of death. This anxiety around dying can be either the fear of pain and suffering or the fear of the end of life and no longer being alive.

Some define life by existence and yet is existence enough in itself for something to be classed as alive? Rocks, streams, rivers, and mountains exist, but are they alive? They may contain life and may operate within a function, but perhaps they themselves are not alive – they are simply present.

Another definition of life is 'to be living'. This opens the definition up to lots of interpretations – from scientific measures of a heartbeat or brain activity to questions over the quality of person's life. The Bible challenges such definitions and perspectives on life and death. Death is not the end of physical life, nor, when considering the spiritual nature of a person, is it necessarily an event. Spiritual death is a process and a state of being.

Last session, we explored Ezekiel 37. In this chapter, often entitled 'The Valley of Dry Bones', we read of an army long since dead. God challenges this seemingly conclusive situation and it quickly becomes no barrier to His will. The passage tells of tendons and flesh being regrown, but this was not enough for them to be alive; breath was needed to breathe into them that 'they may live'. In the resurrection of Jesus, we see another example of God challenging human understanding of what it means to being alive, not just physically but eternally. Luke 24:6 says, 'He is not here, He has risen!' The power of God moved Jesus from a place of death, from a tomb symbolic of an end, to a place of life represented by a purposeless stone laid aside. Through this action, God offered all of His creation a spiritual shift into a position of a new, eternal life with Him (Rom. 6:4).

There are other ways that Christians use the term being 'alive'. A church that is living out the commission to be and make disciples, that gathers together to seek His face and then goes to do His work, that bears fruit and grows is often called 'alive'. Such churches experience a fullness, not regarding space or seating, but in their experience of God and recognition and fulfilment of their call, their vocation, their purpose. As Jesus taught in John 10:10, 'The thief comes only to steal and kill and destroy; I have come that they may have life, and have it to the full.' It is not enough simply to be able to stand and have a body; Jesus offers a life of abundance. This fullness of life is found in the receiving of the Holy Spirit into Christians just as the believers received the Spirit at Pentecost.

In 1 Corinthians 3:16, Paul asks, 'Don't you know that you yourselves are God's temple and that God's Spirit lives among you?' and continues in Romans 8:10, 'But if Christ is in you, then even though your body is subject to death because of sin, the Spirit gives life'. Paul is teaching that as we are reclaimed for God and repaired by God, we can become alive *in* Him, through faith in Jesus and by receiving His breath, the Holy Spirit. This teaching is for the many who are in fear of death, and yet do not know that they are not even alive. Life is needed for an individual to exist, but in Christ fullness of life is offered and through discipleship the Church too is alive.

## Discussion Starters

1. Is living simply having the ability to breathe, to have a pulse or brain function?

2. Do we need a sense of being happy in order to be truly alive?

3. What do you believe, personally, it means to be alive?

4. At what moment did the army of dry bones become alive?

5. What is the difference between being alive and being alive in Christ?

BE ALIVE

6. What is the difference between mercy and grace? How have these gifts from God allowed for life?

7. How is the Holy Spirit necessary to be truly alive?

8. In Romans 6:8–11, we are told to be dead to sin. What does this mean?

9. How does this death to sin lead to life?

10. How can we know we are alive in the Holy Spirit?

## Personal Application

If you have faith in Jesus as Lord then you are saved, but are you truly alive? Prayerfully examine yourself, using the following questions as a guide:

1. Do I worship God before all things?
2. Do I pray and seek His face, His plan and purpose for me?
3. Have I allowed myself to be reclaimed by God as one of His own?
4. Have I identified the areas of my life that require God's repair?
5. Have I received the Spirit into my life?
6. Do I desire the fullness of life Jesus has offered?

## Seeing Jesus in the Scriptures

Jesus brought life. He resurrected people during his ministry; Lazarus (John 11:1–44), Jairus' daughter (Luke 8:49–56), the son of the widow in Nain (Luke 7:11–17). But life does not just mean having a heartbeat. Jesus gave life to those who were not experiencing it due to illness, for example the paralysed man who, once healed, was able to walk, work and worship (Mark 2:1–12). The greatest example of Jesus giving life is through His death. He took on punishment to ensure humankind was saved from death and offered us eternal life (Col. 2:13–15).

WEEK SEVEN
# Awaken others

## Opening Exercise

A testimony of faith often has three sections; 'before knowing Jesus', 'meeting Jesus' and 'since meeting Jesus'. These 'origin' stories are often the basis for sharing experienced faith and if reflected upon often can become effective tools for evangelism. Using these headings, continue to work on writing your short testimony. If anyone has a finished testimony, they might like to share it if there is time.

## Bible Readings

- Isaiah 61:1–2
- Mark 5:18–20
- Acts 9:1–19
- Acts 22:2–6
- Acts 26

## Key Verse

'Go home to your own people and tell them how much the Lord has done for you, and how he has had mercy on you' (Mark 5:19).

## Focus

The need to recognise our own 'origin story' and explore how others can be awakened because of it.

## Opening Our Eyes

Being awakened could be defined as the waking up from one place into a new place, so receiving a new realisation about yourself, your life and the wider connections you have with creation. It has the potential to change your outlook and approach to life and existence as well as your interactions with others with whom you share your life, home, street, community, nation and even planet.

Salvation is the first spiritual awakening, as it brings with it a new beginning, a new you. It is the realisation of the truth in the big story. God created you (Ps. 139:13), He has a plan for you (Jer. 29:11), you have sinned (Rom. 3:23), God wants to forgive you (Ps. 86:5), God has sent Jesus to die for your sins (1 Tim. 1:15), if you accept Jesus as your saviour (Eph. 2:8), you are forgiven and made holy (Heb. 10:10), Jesus rose from the dead (Mark 16:6) and you have the promise of eternal life (John 10:27–28). 2 Corinthians 5:17 reads 'Therefore, if anyone is in Christ, the new creation has come: the old has gone, the new is here!' This is the impact of faith in Jesus as the Christ, the acceptance of the God's mercy in His removal of our justified punishment and the blessing of His grace in giving us the reward of eternal life with Him in the kingdom of Heaven.

Testimonies generally tell of this moment of awakening, the 'meeting Jesus' moment. In Acts 9, we read of the moment of awakening in the life of Paul. Before knowing Jesus, Saul had been present at the stoning of Stephen (Acts 7:58) and was an active persecutor of Christians (Acts 8:1–5). As a Roman citizen (Saul held certain rights and privileges, which he used to his

## AWAKEN OTHERS

advantage when he acquired support to actively seek out and destroy communities of those in the early Church, those who followed 'The Way' (Acts 9:2). Then on a road to Damascus, Saul had his experience of meeting Jesus, who clearly identified himself (Acts 9:5). For three days Saul was blind, humbled by his condition and, seeking to have his sight regained, he followed Christ's instruction to find Ananias to help him. Once healed, 'He got up and was baptised' (Acts 9:18). After meeting Jesus, Saul was forced to lay aside his feeling of hatred and distrust, as well as his ideas of status and authority. From an earthly perspective, Paul had lost all things (Phil. 3:8) but from a spiritual viewpoint, Paul had gained salvation through Jesus, gifting to be used by the Holy Spirit and a new identity, purpose and value in God.

Paul understood the power of his testimony and used it to evangelise. When arrested in Jerusalem, Paul asked to speak to the crowd and shared his meeting with Jesus (Acts 22:2–6). Then in Acts 26, when he was taken before Agrippa, he shared his testimony. Agrippa asked: 'Do you think you can make me a Christian in such a short time?', to which Paul replied, 'Short time or long, I pray to God that not only you but all who are listening to me today may become what I am, except for these chains' (Acts 26:28–29).

Paul went on to travel around ten thousand miles evangelising, planting at least fourteen churches and writing thirteen books of the Bible. Paul had been awakened and went on to journey through the process of humbling, seeking, being reclaimed, being repaired and being made alive in Jesus. In part, it was the sharing of this process, his 'origin story' that brought others to faith also.

## Discussion Starters

1. What is meant by being alive?

2. What is meant by being spiritually awakened?

3. What makes Paul's testimony so powerful?

4. What are the similarities between your story and Paul's?

5. How could others be encouraged by your story?

AWAKEN OTHERS

6. Where and with whom could you share your story?

7. Who might you share your story with?

8. How might your story need different emphasis for different people?

9. Why do you think Agrippa asked if Paul was trying to convert him?

10. Do Christians have to evangelise? Discuss.

## Personal Application

Considering that the process of being awakened is one of the first stages in faith, it perhaps seems strange that this is the last theme of the study. However, the example of revivals throughout history have shown that when Christians are revived in their faith, gifting and commission, there is a ripple effect that brings about an awakening of faith in others. It seems to go hand in hand that a revived Christian will bring about faith in others, as they become an instrument of God's work.

How will you do this? The process of revival of your own faith brings about a recognition of the work of God in your life, in the highs and lows. Such a story can be shared through witness and testimony, just as in the life and ministry of Paul.

## Seeing Jesus in the Scriptures

In Mark 5 Jesus healed a demon-possessed man. As Jesus went to get into a boat, the healed man wanted to go with Jesus. Jesus replied, 'Go home to your own people and tell them how much the Lord has done for you, and how he has had mercy on you' (v19). Jesus did not send him off to strangers, but to his home, which provides us with an example of where to start the process ourselves. Jesus told him to go and tell his story of how he encountered Jesus and what had changed since. The man did this and 'all the people were amazed' (v20). They were suddenly filled with wonder, recognising they were hearing something remarkable. In this moment, they were being told about Jesus' work in the man's life and the potential to have their lives touched.

# Leader's Notes

This series of studies is focused on the biblical process of revival. Though reference may be made to revivals, the revivals in history are not the focus. Nor is this Study Guide 'seven steps to bring about revival'. Revival comes from God and cannot be forced by human intervention, though a desire for revival and a willingness to have one's own personal faith transformed is often the beginning. The sessions follow a suggested pattern of icebreaker, feedback, opening reflections, reading scriptures and discussion, ending with personal application for how the session will have an impact on behaviour and with specific reference to Jesus' ministry. The leader's discretion should be used as you choose the elements you feel would benefit the group in the time available.

It would be useful to read the Bible passages before completing the discussion starter questions, though the passages could be read as you complete the questions if you prefer. The verses from 2 Chronicles 7:11–22 provide the foundation for the first three sessions so specific focus on this passage could be encouraged to link the sessions together.

## **WEEK ONE:** Humble Themselves

**Focus:** The need to humble ourselves before God heals the land.

Session one explores being made humble through identifying a shortcoming in ourselves, as opposed to being humbled by the actions of others. This could be made clear in the feedback from the Opening Exercise and further developed in the Opening our Eyes text.

### Discussion Starters

**1.** This question is aimed at encouraging personal sharing; it may provide an opportunity for a closer fellowship, or may need a closer fellowship to be done comfortably. The judgement of the leader would be needed to decide if it will be helpful to utilise this question and, if so, how to invite people to share. The responses may need clarifying as to how they reflect a sensation of being humbled.

**2.** 1 Kings 6 and 2 Chronicles 7 may be useful in approaching this question as they reveal the commitment and submission of Solomon to God's will and a greater power. Solomon prioritised the building of the Temple before that of the palace.

**3.** This question seeks to prompt specific examples in modern-day life based upon the inspiration of David and Solomon in their journeys with God. Generally, answers may follow a desire to be made low before God and submit to his will and then, because of that, any action will be motivated and directed by God's kingdom plan, not those of an individual.

**4.** This question relates to Romans 3:23 and may provoke some exploration and reflection. It could be supported by additional questioning, such as: What are the challenges in accepting this? Why is it important to recognise the sin in our lives? What is the impact of unrepented sin?

## LEADER'S NOTES

**5.** Psalm 105:4 may be used to emphasise the importance of the action. God's face is often interpreted as His presence. James 4:8 outlines that seeking God's presence can be done through prayer, confession and seeking to build a relationship with him through abandoning a loyalty to the world. In essence, humbling ourselves. God has revealed himself in many ways, e.g. through creation, the Holy Spirit, the Word and through Jesus.

**6.** The connection here is the recognition of one's own sin combined with a desire to repent being a necessary prerequisite to receiving forgiveness. The humbling process puts a spotlight on our own sins and enables the process to begin in full awareness. The verses from 2 Chronicles 7 outline this necessary conditional aspect of the process.

**7.** The next step from humbling oneself and seeking forgiveness is the transformation that occurs to create a person who is more forgiving of others. This is reflected in the behaviours of Jesus outlined in Philippians 2:3–11 and is expected of the believers as the passage continues in verse 12–13.

**8.** These questions should hopefully aid reflection on the impact of being humbled on people as stewards of creation and disciples of Jesus. Examples of answers may include: conflict, famine, persecution and disasters. Suggested responses may be: charitable giving of money, resources and time, advocacy and a readiness to support. The process of being humbled will ensure an equality between those who serve and those who are being served.

The process of being humbled must be fuelled by a sincere desire for a closer relationship with God and a willing evaluation of a life lived against the teaching of the Bible. The final part of this week's session provides a list of reflective statements to support a person who is seeking to initiate this process in their own life. There are also some short questions to support this evaluation and identify the need for one to be humbled in preparation for a revival of faith through the Holy Spirit.

## WEEK TWO: Pray and Seek

**Focus:** The need to become a prayerful people before God heals the land.

This session continues the initial theme of seeking a change within a person's behaviour. The verses from 2 Chronicles are looked at again and built upon as the session explores the next stage of behavioural change God expects of those seeking revival.

The theme is prayer and its role as the natural next step in revival and the desire for God's will and way to become clear. Prayer is not simply a form of communication with God but a way to develop a deeper relationship with God; in revival times, this is provoked by a period of humbling and confession. It is hoped that the icebreaker will reveal this theme but the leader may want to make the connection more explicit depending on the points and experiences shared by the group.

### Discussion Starters
**1.** The first question makes a reference to what follows from prayer – the desire to see God's will and way made clear for His people to serve and follow. Prayer is a key step in developing that closeness with God from which these things are revealed. Without the foundation of prayer, an individual may not be as prepared to study, surrender and serve with clarity.

**2.** Prayerful people tend to hold some common characteristics. They are devout in their approach to prayer, perhaps observing a rhythm to their prayer pattern. They are earnest in their recognition of the power of prayer and understand that prayer transcends the limitations of the physical and opens up

LEADER'S NOTES

opportunities for the spiritual. Finally, they are sincere in the act of prayer, not simply going through the motions or seeking to appear prayerful.

**3.** 'O Lord…' used by Habakkuk suggests a longing that the prophet has; a deep desire for what he asks of God. This longing could be a developed desperation, which has been present over a period of time. Also, there is a focus which suggests that what is being asked for can only come from God.

**4.** Habakkuk outlines all the reasons why revival is needed. There is almost a negative tone to his prayer as he dwells on the problems. Habakkuk then announces that even in such difficulties, he can 'rejoice in the Lord'. It is in God that he finds strength, guidance and prosperity.

**5.** Similarities can be seen between the psalm and the prayer of Habakkuk as they both illustrate our need and recognise God's power to meet that need. Also, both recognise the work of God they have heard or observed in similar circumstances in the past and therefore have reassurance that God can and will act.

**6.** This question will have personal responses, but aims to recognise the shift in focus from our will to His. This usually comes with maturity of faith but can also be impacted upon by the emotional state of the person praying and where they are in the processing of their own experience.

**7.** A longing for God's plan to be realised is often illustrated in behaviours of prayer, fasting, a discerning of next steps in desire for His direction and a commitment to be used by Him. This could be presented publicly in a congregational act of response and corporate time of prayer, perhaps declaring 'Here am I, send me' (Isa. 6:8).

**8.** Following the biblical call for humility, prayer and seeking already explored, prayers of confession and repentance, prayer for a willingness to be renewed in faith, prayers for a passionate approach to prayer, prayers for a revealing of new approaches to prayer, prayers for the Holy Spirit to guide, counsel and gift, prayers for God to lay a new vision on the church community.

The session ends with some questions for personal reflection. They could be discussed in the session or explored separately by people in their own quiet time.

## **WEEK THREE:** And Turn Away

**Focus:** The need to acknowledge sin, confess and repent.

The theme of seeking a change in the individual continues in session three as the last part of this aspect of exploration. The icebreaker seeks to reveal life-changing moments and the impact these have had a on a person. The leader will need to facilitate this sharing well to keep the focus on the positive change to the individual as a person. This will lay the foundation for exploration as to how change, though not always easy, can provoke positive results in the future.

The change being explored in this session regards the change to step away from sin. This is the next step following the recognition of sin and the seeking of forgiveness for sins committed. This is the necessary move towards repentance and the transformation of oneself as a result of forgiveness in Jesus. The notes open up the focus and may provide a time of reflection before enquiry.

### **Discussion Starters**
**1.** It may be useful to share people's own definitions of sin and then to find a dictionary definition of sin. It may read something along the lines of sin being the breaking of religious law. James 4:17 describes sin as not doing what is known as right, while 1 John 3:4 describes sin as lawlessness – the law in this case

## LEADER'S NOTES

being God's Word. A good start for examples in the Bible would be the actions prohibited in the Ten Commandments such as lying, adultery, murder.

**2.** Adam and Eve broke God's law and were punished (Gen. 3). The punishment was the removal of God's provision, and the need for them to work hard in order to survive. (Their work before this point had been to take care of the needs of the garden, while God took care of their needs.) The worst thing was that they would no longer be in close relationship with God, no longer able to walk with him in Eden. Their sinful behaviour did not just have an impact on them though; it went further and would impact upon their children's relationship with God. The same could be said for sin today. It prevents people from having a close relationship with God and one another. For example, embracing sin has a negative impact on how a person teaches and encourages others to enter into a relationship with God.

**3.** God gave His commandments (Exod. 20:1–17) in response to sinfulness. There is nothing in the Bible to suggest they no longer apply. Jesus condensed the teaching of them (Matt. 22:34-40) into loving God (one God, no idols, no swearing using His name, keeping the Sabbath) and loving each other (honour your parents, don't kill, no committing adultery, no stealing, no lying, no jealousy).

**4.** The discussion shared regarding Adam and Eve can be revisited here, especially the point on the distance created between humankind and God as a consequence of sin. Also, reference could be made to Romans 3:23 and Romans 6:23 here, concluding that sin results in death.

**5.** A willingness to step away is needed and this is provoked by knowledge of understanding what it means to remain in sin and the positives of stepping out of that position of sin. The willingness and understanding of the necessity to shift one's life needs to become evident in action. Reminding ourselves that following God's law results in His love (John 14:21) is a powerful constant in the process.

**6.** In Colossians 3:5, Paul tells us to put to death those things which are of the earth. It is necessary to guard oneself in the sinful world in order that one may be in the world but not of it (John 17:13–19). Paul also asserts that we should train ourselves for godliness (1 Tim. 4:7) and be imitators of God (Eph. 5:1–20). Therefore, to be in the world but not of it requires a perseverance and disciplined approach to our behaviours; restricting our interactions with temptation (Mark 9:42–50), wearing the armour of God (Eph. 6:14–18) and keeping short accounts when we fall (1 John 1:9).

**7.** It may be useful to consider the separation of sin and the individual; teaching about sin while not teaching about a person's specific sin. The Holy Spirit will bring a person close to God; finger-pointing often has the opposite effect. Also, the timing of the teaching is key. Displaying love is a useful foundation to teach on sin from as it helps to remove the feeling of judgement. With trust already established people are more open to being taught and challenged.

**8.** Some people do not know what is sinful, so identifying what is sin in the world would be helpful. Then you could explore the impact of committing such sins. (See question six for specifics.) The pastoral support of the church alongside established, Spirit-filled prayer ministry would be of great use to someone going through the process.

The group session ends with a reflection on how Jesus experienced temptation. We should be reassured by this. We have a saviour who knows what it is like to be human. Jesus gave us a model of how to approach temptation.

Also provided are a series of steps that could benefit some. They cannot be done as a quick fix and are more of an embedding process requiring time to establish rhythm and devotion. The impact of these may be immediate but the process is challenging and requires perseverance.

## WEEK FOUR: Be Reclaimed

**Focus:** God wants to reclaim His creation through the cross of Jesus.

The focus moves now from us seeking to bring about a change in our character, behaviour and will to accepting God making a change in us. The icebreaker is focused on seeing potential and value in things where others/society perhaps has given up and thrown out.

The Opening Our Eyes section makes the contrast between the values seen in objects and that seen in people. The verses for this week teach the value of God's people, His creation and how that value is intrinsic. The clear and consistent repetition in this teaching of value throughout Scripture reflects the lack of this understanding among humanity.

God is creator, but through accepting the power of fashions, fads, peer pressures and social accountability, we seem to hand over our ownership to another. A person's value has become based upon the measure of other people. Value is now based on the current social measures rather than the intrinsic value found as a child of God.

People who are absorbed into this social measure of value, those who have stepped away from God, require an act of reclamation on their return. Just as the father of the prodigal son never stopped being his father, the son still needed that moment where the father ran to him and embraced him as an act of reclamation. For Christians, that action was in the crucifixion of Jesus but can be affirmed in renewed, Spirit-fuelled faith. It is worth making the point that a person could have stepped away in their heart and still attend church, Bible study, prayer meetings etc without anyone knowing what is going on inside.

**Discussion Starters**

**1.** Reclamation could be described using examples of those found in the Opening Our Eyes section as well as making reference to current television programmes that seek to take previously undervalued items and give them fresh meaning and value. Generally, it is the claiming of something back; in this sense God can reclaim his people (Isa. 11:11 illustrates this).

**2.** There are many things that cause a person to seek new ownership. Negative experience of church and Christians can turn a person away from God; people experiencing disappointment and difficulties while on a journey of faith can lead them to become disheartened and therefore step away, the distractions provided from society can catch their attention, being isolated and doubting, having sinful desires and living/working/studying a distance away from the church community can also lead them away.

**3.** It would be understandable to blame Adam and Eve (Gen. 3) or even the serpent for the sin in the world and many would agree that Satan is at the root of all evil (John 8:44). However, attributing blame is not a fruit-bearing behaviour. Romans 2:1 says, 'You, therefore, have no excuse'; judging others for sin is hypocritical as we have all sinned. We are responsible for our own sin (Gal. 6:5).

**4.** Matthew 5:16 explains that others will know who your father is by your behaviour. 'In the same way, let your light shine before others, that they may see your good deeds and glorify your Father in heaven.' Conversely, sinful behaviour reflects that of Satan, the 'god of this age' (2 Cor. 4:4).

## LEADER'S NOTES

**5.** The first part of this discussion will be based upon personal reflection and people may or may not want to share as they feel comfortable. In response to how to find out God's plan, it may be useful to ask people to share how they have had this revealed to them. The Bible tells us that we should ask (Jas 1:5), wait (Psa. 27:14), be willing to submit to His plan (Isa. 6:8) and recognise God's plan for us may be different from His plan for others (1 Pet. 4:10). Also, ask the group to reflect on how God has already gifted or used them. What experiences has each one had that He may want them to gain from in order to walk the path He has laid? You might find it helpful to take time to read and consider Romans 8:28 too.

**6.** Leviticus 11:24-28 repeats the phrase, 'unclean until evening'. The time spent in sin is only ever temporary. God's desire is that we return to Him. Since the creation of the world, God has been creating opportunities for closeness with His people. The garden, the rainbow, the tribes, the exodus, the priesthood, the throne and the cross are all illustrations of God's desire to reclaim His people from the 'god of this age' and also illustrate the choice that people have and always have had: to return to God – or not. Reference has already been made to the prodigal son. You could make the point explicit that it was the choice of the son to leave and the choice of the son to return. We can imagine how the father felt and consider all the pieces of advice and discouragement he could have given the son and yet the father let him go. However, the father was also ready to receive him on his return. The actions of the father were enough to wipe away the traces of the mistakes made and reassert value.

**7.** At Pentecost the Holy Spirit fell upon the earth. The Holy Spirit was present at the beginning of time (Gen. 1:2) when He hovered over the waters of the earth. The power of God cannot be restricted or corseted, and yet, when the Spirit fell on the day of Pentecost His power did not cover the earth, or a country or even a city – it was restricted to one room. Why? That room was the only space that contained those whose faith, commitment and identity as follows of Jesus made them ready to receive. We must make the step away from the world, to take a step closer to the kingdom of God.

**8.** Facilitate an open discussion as to how people's lives changed when they came to faith. Particular focus could be given as to how their behaviours, outlook and relationships with others changed.

Reflection on the last question in the Personal Application section would be a good way to finish off the session. Try to step away from the academic here and encourage people to personalise their answer so that they leave with the assurance of the value gained in God's reclamation of them.

## WEEK FIVE: Be Repaired

**Focus:** We return to God broken, but he can repair the broken.

We return to God needing repair. In a world built on consumption, repair is not something people often do. These days it is often easier and cheaper to buy new. Therefore, repair only takes place when something has meaning or personal, rather than monetary, value. The feedback from the icebreaker will hopefully illustrate this point (do make it clear if not).

The Opening Our Eyes section makes connections between the Japanese practice of 'kintsugi' and God repairing us. It would be useful to find a video clip online or even pictures to show this process and make the illustration a little clearer – a quick internet search for 'kintsugi' should give you plenty of examples to choose from.

**Discussion Starters:**
**1.** Brokenness may be seen in a person's inability to function spiritually, emotionally or practically. A person may have lost

## LEADER'S NOTES

their ability to reason and be rational and their life starts to reflect this through changed behaviours. However, a person could be broken and not display anything that reveals that fact. They may internalise their brokenness and continue to function unchanged. There are many stories of Christians who lost their anchor in the faith and continued to attend church etc without anyone knowing.

**2.** While there are some things that can be damaged so much they seem to be beyond repair, this does depend on the one seeking to mend the object; their desire to find pieces that are missing, their knowledge of the object before it was broken, their patience to invest the time, their skill in the work needed and their ability to see value in the object. As regards God, He has the desire, knowledge, patience, skill and sees the value in all the brokenness to take on the repair work in our lives.

**3.** The brokenness of the prodigal son (Luke 15:11–32) became evident the moment the son asked for his share of his inheritance. The father could have acted then and highlighted the problem but the reparation could not be made until the son desired it and was in a position to recognise the brokenness within himself. The son was the one who started the repair work by returning; the father then simply completed the process. If we apply this in broader terms to God's work of repair, there will be a time of waiting and a self-initiated act of reparation before God acts.

**4.** Kintsugi gathers the pieces of an object and puts them back so that the cracks are repaired, but also in a way that causes those cracks to be celebrated as a part of its existence. This is not a celebration of the breaking or the crack but a celebration of the repair and the fact the item can be used for its purpose again. God does the same for us, not just repairing us but ensuring we can meet our purpose again (Luke 5:17–26). More detail is explored in the next question.

**5.** The repairs God has brought about in our lives as Christians are celebrated in our testimony. It is a vehicle for praise but also a great way to witness. We see examples in Scripture of testimony being used to celebrate God's reparation of us but also to illustrate that the individual is about to meet their purpose again. Paul often shared his testimony as celebration of God's repair work on him (see Acts 22).

**6.** God raised the bones to illustrate that nothing is beyond reparation and resurrection. This action also reflects that those who act in His name can see His power working through them. The revived army represented God's chosen people and His promise to revive them.

**7.** God used Ezekiel as a conduit for His power to move and be active. Ezekiel was a prophet and therefore was a mouthpiece for the Lord.

**8.** The bones rattled, then came together, tendons and skin covered them, but there was no breath in them. God breathed His breath into them and then they stood up and were alive.

**9.** Discuss, at what point did they come alive? The physical reparation was meaningless until God breathed into them; God explains that His breath is His Spirit. Without the Holy Spirit we are not alive.

**10.** Read Isaiah 44:1-5. Verse 5 states that people will say that they belong to the Lord. God says that this will be because they believe God is the one who created them and He is the one who provides for them. This phrase appears again in Romans 14:8. Paul says that people who say that they belong to the Lord will behave in a certain way.

When we explore the ministry of Jesus there were several miracles performed that repaired people physically. It is worth exploring, though, how the life of the person changed from that physical reparation. At the time of Christ, those with physical disabilities were not permitted to worship in the temple (Lev. 21:16-23). So the reparation that took place provided both physical and spiritual repair. The crucifixion and the tearing of the curtain provided the ultimate moment of repair to the relationship between God and humankind (Luke 23:45). One way to celebrate the repairs God has made to an individual's life is for them to share their testimony. It may be a good idea to ask members of the group to craft a personal testimony after the session, focusing on how they came to know God, although they will also be given an opportunity at the start of session seven to do this.

## WEEK SIX: Be Alive

**Focus:** Being able to stand, to move and to walk is not the same as being alive.

For the icebreaker, ask for group members to share moments when they felt alive. Use the questions to dig deeper and get more detail from those who feel comfortable to share. What are the common features of people's experiences? These may be a real sense of joy, of identity, of risk or of purpose. This session explores what it means to be alive in society today and the challenge the Bible makes to society's definitions.

The session tackles some complex aspects of the Christian faith so you may want to read through all the verses together and keep referring back to them.

### Discussion Starters
**1.** From the reflection passage there are examples to draw upon to illustrate that more is needed to be alive. Members of the group may provide more examples, which may include personal experiences of the struggles of people who had the basic function of life without being alive.

**2.** Happiness is not necessarily an indication of being alive. There are examples in Scripture of those who lamented but were alive in God. Job is a great example to share if the discussion moves to it. Grief and pain are also useful processes to experience to ensure a value for life and deeper perspective on what it mean to be alive.

**3.** This answer is subjective and is for personal sharing. You may wish to pose the question and then answer it themselves to allow people time to consider their own point of view. You could bring the sharing together with the point that a person could live their life and not be alive in Christ.

**4.** The army came alive once they had received God's breath. God goes on to refer to His breath as His Spirit. The army came alive because they received the Holy Spirit. Before this point their bones attached and tendons, flesh and skin were growing but yet, they were still dead even though the flesh lived.

**5.** Romans 6:8–11 provides an answer to this question, and it would be useful to read the surrounding verses, if not the whole chapter. If it isn't said by anyone, do point out that Christ gives new life. Those who have died in Christ have also been resurrected in Him to a new life. As it says in Romans 6:23, they have gained eternal life from God.

**6.** Mercy is not giving a punishment when it is deserved. Grace is giving a reward when it is not deserved. By God's mercy in the crucifixion of Jesus, humankind need not receive the punishment they deserve as sinners. Through God's grace humankind is offered the gift of eternal life. Faith in Jesus as saviour is the only prerequisite (Rom. 10:9).

**7.** In John 6:63, Jesus said, 'The Spirit gives life'. In Ezekiel 37 it is the Spirit that gives life to the army. Therefore, it doesn't not matter how long a person has been dead, literally or spiritually, the Spirit can pour out life afresh upon them.

LEADER'S NOTES

**8.** To be dead to sin means to not be a living host to sinfulness. Being dead will prevent temptation to sin but also prevent sin from having a place to reside and therefore control. By giving ourselves as a living sacrifice to God, by belonging to Him, we aim to remove our own sinful ways and give ourselves to God as our master, no longer to be mastered by the sin in the world.

**9.** In a continuation of the previous question's discussion, sin is a barrier to life. Genesis 3 teaches how sin can create a barrier between humankind and God. Sin can destroy relationships. Death to sin therefore leads to relationship with God. Without a relationship with God we cannot be truly alive. Relationship with God is secured through the death of Jesus. Relationship with God is maintained through the power of the Holy Spirit.

**10.** Once we acknowledge Jesus as saviour, we receive the Holy Spirit and become a vessel (1 Cor. 3:16). The Spirit then provides guidance, counsel and convicts us of our sin and temptation to sin (John 16:8). Our lives are transformed and we have a new life (Titus 3:5). The Spirit convicts us to witness to others (Acts 1:8). Those who are filled with the Spirit will bear fruit (Gal. 5:22–23), all for the glory of God (John 15:8).

Throughout the earthly ministry of Jesus, people were given literal life, raised again from death. Jesus also gave spiritual life in the healing of people, enabling them to worship fully. These two aspects of His ministry were combined in the act of the crucifixion and resurrection. One to give spiritual life and allow people to die to sin free from punishment, the other to give life eternally in the kingdom of Heaven.

The set of questions within the Personal Application section could be completed after the session for people to evaluate their own spiritual life and how they are alive. You may feel it is appropriate to read them through and then open up a time of prayer.

## **WEEK 7:** Awaken Others

**Focus:** The need to recognise our own 'origin story' and explore how others can be awakened because of it.

This is the final session of the study. It focuses on reaching out to others, and bringing about awakening in them. Testimony plays a part in this process.

It would be good to ask people to look at the icebreaker before the session to give them time to work on their testimony. If people feel they would like to share in depth, you may want to have a session simply for fellowship and sharing testimonies in addition to the set sessions; though such a session is not planned for in this study series it is facilitated through this final session.

If people have not been able to prepare a testimony it would still be helpful for them to think about how they would tell their own story, as it will make it easier for them to share it with others in the future.

### Discussion Starters

**1.** This is a recap to last week to link the two sessions together. If needed check the leader's notes from the previous session.

**2.** Spiritual awakenings are often a revelation to a new spiritual truth. In Christianity the primary spiritual awakening is the realisation that Jesus is Lord and that through the crucifixion there is salvation. The Opening Our Eyes section provides a detailed answer to this with verses to look at and discuss.

**3.** This will impact upon people differently so it is worth providing space for people to explore and share how it moves them, and to think about where they see the power at work. For some it may be in the complete transformation of his life, in terms of his role in society, work, status in a community, title in

## LEADER'S NOTES

religion, how and where he lived etc. For others it may be the miracle of encountering Jesus and being healed.

**4.** This is for individuals to answer. You may want to answer this question first to provide others with time to share. Hopefully people will have read through the questions before the session and be prepared.

**5.** Often, people are touched by seeing themselves in another story. They are then able to recognise the emotions and challenges particular experiences have brought. The encouragement comes in the realisation of salvation and continued care from, and relationship with, God.

**6.** Paul was chained to a guard for a couple of years while under house arrest in Rome. It is likely the guard changed over time so he would have had the opportunity to share his story with various guards. Ask people: Where do you spend your time? Then get individuals to think about those people they interact with regularly, and to also think about those people that may have been unnoticed by them but God could be calling them to reach out to and eventually tell their story to.

**7.** Here are some follow-on question prompts for you to aid discussion if necessary. Which aspects of your origin story are quite specific to certain people? Who may struggle with your story? Maybe your story is specific to a particular group in society, which could be a sign of your call to reach that group?

**8.** Could it have been that Agrippa was beginning to be moved by the story and he was trying to stop the process? Maybe it was that Paul was so passionate in his sharing that it was obvious Paul wanted Agrippa to believe.

**9.** The short answer is yes. The great commission calls all disciples to, 'Therefore go and make disciples of all nations, baptising them in the name of the Father and of the Son and of the Holy Spirit' (Matt. 28:19). The act of baptism is not just about adjusting how people behave. It is a move in a person's beliefs that leads to baptism. It is also worth noting that there is a variety of ministries in the Church (1 Cor. 12:5) to fulfil the commission.

When encouraging people to interaction with the Personal Application section, you could also suggest they consider the possible ways they have been revived during the course of the study and how they believe their own revival may be used to bring about awakening in others. It is the last session, but, as suggested, it may be useful to have an additional opportunity to share your testimonies with each other, or even with the wider church.

# Daily Guide

This daily guide is designed to help you to engage with the material in the Study Guide in between the sessions. Start this two days before your first session. More copies of this daily guide are available to download for free from **wvly.org/c2ccv**.

| | |
|---|---|
| **Day 1** | Read: 2 Chronicles 7:11–22, John 3:30, Romans 3:23, Philippians 2:3–11, 1 Peter 5:6. |
| **Day 2** | Pray: O Lord, open my heart and mind to receive from you and be humbled. |
| **Day 3** | Consider: Has there been a time when I felt humbled? What caused this? |
| **Day 4** | Read through Week One in the Study Guide. |
| **Day 5** | Reflect: How can I be made low so that I may lift God high? |
| **Day 6** | Ask: O Lord, make me your servant that I may direct all glory to you. |
| **Day 7** | Act: Plan a way to selflessly serve others this week. |
| **Day 8** | Read: 2 Chronicles 7:11–22, Habakkuk, Psalm 80, Psalm 85:1–7. |
| **Day 9** | Pray: O Lord, let me desire revival in myself and your creation. |
| **Day 10** | Consider: Has there been a time when you have felt a desperate need to pray? |
| **Day 11** | Read through Week Two in the Study Guide. |

**Day 12** Reflect: How can I remove distractions so that I may come closer to God?

**Day 13** Ask: O Lord, reveal your plan and path for me, that I may follow.

**Day 14** Act: Find some time in the week to simply be in God's presence.

**Day 15** Read: Genesis 3, Exodus 20:1–17, 2 Chronicles 7:11–22, John 14:21, Acts 3:19.

**Day 16** Pray: O Lord, help me to see how you have worked, and continue to work, in my life.

**Day 17** Consider: What major changes have I had in my life?

**Day 18** Read through Week Three in the Study Guide.

**Day 19** Reflect: What parts of my life do I need to turn away from?

**Day 20** Ask: O Lord, help me to turn to you in every part of my life.

**Day 21** Act: Write a list of repeated sins in your life.

**Day 22** Read: Psalm 139:13–18, Luke 15:11–32, Acts 16:31, Ephesians 1:4–5, 1 Peter 2:9.

**Day 23** Pray: O Lord, I confess my sins, especially those I repeat.

**Day 24** Consider: Have you ever bought anything second-hand? What was it that attracted you to it?

**Day 25** Read through Week Four in the Study Guide.

**Day 26** Reflect: How can I be a steward of creation, including caring for myself?

**Day 27** Ask: O Lord, help me to recognise the times when I feel closest to you.

**Day 28** Act: Plan the rhythm of your devotions. When do you, or could you, pray and study?

**Day 29** Read: Isaiah 44:1–5, Ezekiel 37:1–14, Luke 5:17–26, Luke 8:40–56.

**Day 30** Pray: O Lord, give me discipline to do more of the things that bring me close to you.

**Day 31** Consider: Have you had anything that you have needed to be repaired? Why didn't you just replace it?

**Day 32** Read through Week Five in the Study Guide.

## DAILY GUIDE

| | |
|---|---|
| **Day 33** | Reflect: What parts of me need repair? |
| **Day 34** | Ask: O Lord, repair the parts of me that I have allowed to be broken by sin. |
| **Day 35** | Act: Create some form of art; poetry, painting, song etc. that reflects how you have been repaired. |
| **Day 36** | Read: Luke 24:6, John 1:1–4, John 10:10, Romans 6:3-11. |
| **Day 37** | Pray: O Lord, thank you that through you, I can be repaired and revived. |
| **Day 38** | Consider: Has there ever been a time when you have felt truly alive? |
| **Day 39** | Read through Week Six in the Study Guide. |
| **Day 40** | Reflect: What aspects of your day to day reflect that you are alive? |
| **Day 41** | Ask: O Lord, stir in me a recognition of the precious gift of life I have received from you. |
| **Day 42** | Act: Complete the Personal Application questions from Week Six. |
| **Day 43** | Read: Isaiah 61:1–2, Mark 5:18–20, Acts 9:1–19, Acts 22:2–6, Acts 26. |
| **Day 44** | Pray: O Lord, thank you for the people you used to bring me to faith. Revive my faith in you. |
| **Day 45** | Consider: What was your life like: before knowing Jesus, meeting Jesus, since meeting Jesus? |
| **Day 46** | Read through Week Seven in the Study Guide. |
| **Day 47** | Reflect: How/where has God gifted me to share Jesus with others at the right time in the right way? |
| **Day 48** | Ask: O Lord, call me again, fill me anew, send me once more. In Jesus' name. |
| **Day 49** | Act: Share part of your testimony with someone. |

# The Cover to Cover Bible Study Series

## CHARACTERS

**Abraham**
Adventures of faith
ISBN: 978-1-78259-089-7

**Barnabas**
Son of encouragement
ISBN: 978-1-85345-911-5

**David**
A man after God's own heart
ISBN: 978-1-78259-444-3

**Elijah**
A man and his God
ISBN: 978-1-85345-575-9

**Elisha**
A lesson in faithfulness
ISBN: 978-1-78259-494-9

**Jacob**
Taking hold of God's blessing
ISBN: 978-1-78259-685-1

**Joseph**
The power of forgiveness and reconciliation
ISBN: 978-1-85345-252-9

**Mary**
The mother of Jesus
ISBN: 978-1-78259-402-4

**Moses**
Face to face with God
ISBN: 978-1-85345-336-6

## THEMES

**Bible Genres**
Hearing what the Bible really says
ISBN: 978-1-85345-987-0

**Covenants**
God's promises and their relevance today
ISBN: 978-1-85345-255-0

**The Creed**
Belief in action
ISBN: 978-1-78259-202-0

**The Divine Blueprint**
God's extraordinary power in ordinary lives
ISBN: 978-1-85345-292-5

**Fruit of the Spirit**
Growing more like Jesus
ISBN: 978-1-78951-495-7

**God's Rescue Plan**
Finding God's fingerprints on human history
ISBN: 978-1-85345-294-9

**Great Prayers of the Bible**
Applying them to our lives today
ISBN: 978-1-85345-253-6

**The Holy Spirit**
Understanding and experiencing Him
ISBN: 978-1-85345-254-3

**NEW: I Ams**
Who is Jesus?
ISBN: 978-1-78951-499-5

**The Image of God**
His attributes and character
ISBN: 978-1-85345-228-4

**Names of God**
Exploring the depths of God's character
ISBN: 978-1-85345-680-0

**NEW: Revive Your Church**
Seeking and encountering abundant life
ISBN: 978-1-78951-441-4

**Rivers of Justice**
Responding to God's call to righteousness today
ISBN: 978-1-85345-339-7

**The Second Coming**
Living in the light of Jesus' return
ISBN: 978-1-85345-422-6

**The Uniqueness of our Faith**
What makes Christianity distinctive?
ISBN: 978-1-85345-232-1

**NEW: Violence against Women**
Discovering El Roi, The God Who Sees
ISBN: 978-1-78951-445-2

## NEW TESTAMENT

**NEW: Matthew**
Your Kingdom Come
ISBN: 978-1-78951-450-6

**Mark**
Life as it is meant to be lived
ISBN: 978-1-85345-233-8

**Luke**
A prescription for living
ISBN: 978-1-78259-270-9

**John's Gospel**
Exploring the seven miraculous signs
ISBN: 978-1-85345-295-6

**Acts 1–12**
Church on the move
ISBN: 978-1-85345-574-2

**Acts 13–28**
To the ends of the earth
ISBN: 978-1-85345-592-6

**The Letter to the Romans**
Good news for everyone
ISBN: 978-1-85345-250-5

**1 Corinthians**
Growing a Spirit-filled church
ISBN: 978-1-78951-510-7

**2 Corinthians**
Restoring harmony
ISBN: 978-1-85345-551-3

**Galatians**
Freedom in Christ
ISBN: 978-1-85345-648-0

**Ephesians**
Claiming your inheritance
ISBN: 978-1-85345-229-1

**Philippians**
Living for the sake
of the gospel
ISBN: 978-1-85345-421-9

**The Letter to the Colossians**
In Christ alone
ISBN: 978-1-855345-405-9

**Thessalonians**
Building Church in
changing times
ISBN: 978-1-78259-443-7

**1 Timothy**
Healthy churches –
effective Christians
ISBN: 978-1-85345-291-8

**2 Timothy and Titus**
Vital Christianity
ISBN: 978-1-85345-338-0

**Philemon**
From slavery to freedom
ISBN: 978-1-85345-453-0

**Hebrews**
Jesus – simply the best
ISBN: 978-1-85345-337-3

**James**
Faith in action
ISBN: 978-1-85345-293-2

**1 Peter**
Good reasons for hope
ISBN: 978-1-78259-088-0

**2 Peter**
Living in the light of
God's promises
ISBN: 978-1-78259-403-1

**1,2,3 John**
Walking in the truth
ISBN: 978-1-78951-501-5

**Revelation 1–3**
Christ's call to the Church
ISBN: 978-1-85345-461-5

**Revelation 4–22**
The Lamb wins! Christ's
final victory
ISBN: 978-1-85345-411-0

**The Armour of God**
Living in His strength
ISBN: 978-1-78259-583-0

**The Beatitudes**
Immersed in the grace of Christ
ISBN: 978-1-78259-495-6

**The Lord's Prayer**
Praying Jesus' way
ISBN: 978-1-85345-460-8

**Parables**
Communicating God on earth
ISBN: 978-1-85345-340-3

**Prayers of Jesus**
Hearing His heartbeat
ISBN: 978-1-85345-647-3

**The Prodigal Son**
Amazing grace
ISBN: 978-1-85345-412-7

**The Sermon on the Mount**
Life within the new covenant
ISBN: 978-1-85345-370-0

## OLD TESTAMENT

**Genesis 1–11**
Foundations of reality
ISBN: 978-1-85345-404-2

**Genesis 12–50**
Founding fathers of faith
ISBN: 978-1-78259-960-9

**Exodus**
God's Epic Rescue
ISBN: 978-1-78951-272-4

**The Ten Commandments**
Living God's Way
ISBN: 978-1-85345-593-3

**Joshua 1–10**
Hand in hand with God
ISBN: 978-1-85345-542-7

**Joshua 11–24**
Called to service
ISBN: 978-1-78951-138-3

**Judges 1–8**
The spiral of faith
ISBN: 978-1-85345-681-7

**Judges 9–21**
Learning to live God's way
ISBN: 978-1-85345-910-8

**Ruth**
Loving kindness in action
ISBN: 978-1-85345-231-4

**Nehemiah**
Principles for life
ISBN: 978-1-85345-335-9

**Esther**
For such a time as this
ISBN: 978-1-85345-511-7

**Job**
The source of wisdom
ISBN: 978-1-78259-992-0

**Psalms**
Songs of life
ISBN: 978-1-78951-240-3

**23rd Psalm**
The Lord is my shepherd
ISBN: 978-1-85345-449-3

**Proverbs**
Living a life of wisdom
ISBN: 978-1-85345-373-1

**Ecclesiastes**
Hard questions and
spiritual answers
ISBN: 978-1-78951-508-4

**Song of Songs**
A celebration of love
ISBN: 978-1-78259-959-3

**Isaiah 1–39**
Prophet to the nations
ISBN: 978-1-85345-510-0

**Isaiah 40–66**
Prophet of restoration
ISBN: 978-1-85345-550-6

**Jeremiah**
The passionate prophet
ISBN: 978-1-85345-372-4

**Ezekiel**
A prophet for all times
ISBN: 978-1-78259-836-7

**Daniel**
Living boldly for God
ISBN: 978-1-78951-503-9

**Hosea**
The love that never fails
ISBN: 978-1-85345-290-1

**Joel**
Getting real with God
ISBN: 978-1-78951-927-2

**Jonah**
Rescued from the depths
ISBN: 978-1-78259-762-9

**Habakkuk**
Choosing God's way
ISBN: 978-1-78259-843-5

**Haggai**
Motivating God's people
ISBN: 978-1-78259-686-8

**Zechariah**
Seeing God's bigger picture
ISBN: 978-1-78951-263-2

For current prices or to order, visit **waverleyabbeytrust.org/publishing**